AI Mastery for Everyone

*Learn Practical AI Skills in 7 Days Without Coding
Experience*

Mahmud Huseyin

AI Mastery for Everyone: Learn Practical AI Skills in 7 Days Without Coding Experience

Table of Contents

Introduction: Why Everyone Needs AI Skills Today

Welcome to "AI Mastery for Everyone" – your accessible gateway to the world of artificial intelligence. If you've picked up this book, you're likely curious about AI but perhaps intimidated by what seems like a complex, technical field. Let me reassure you right away: this book is designed specifically for you – someone with no coding experience who wants to harness the incredible power of AI in your everyday life and work.

The AI Revolution is Here

In the last few years, artificial intelligence has moved from research labs and tech companies into our daily lives. It's no longer a futuristic concept – it's present in the phones we use, the entertainment we consume, the shopping recommendations we receive, and increasingly, in the tools we use at work.

According to recent data, the global AI market is expected to reach nearly $200 billion by 2025, growing at an incredible rate of over 35% annually. This explosive growth isn't just affecting technology companies – it's transforming every industry from healthcare and education to retail and finance.

Why Everyone Needs AI Skills Now

You might be wondering: "Why do I need to learn about AI if I'm not a programmer or data scientist?" The answer is simple – in today's rapidly evolving landscape, AI literacy is becoming as essential as digital literacy was a decade ago. Here's why:

1. **Staying Relevant in the Workforce**: By 2024, an estimated 65% of application development will be done using low-code and no-code platforms, making AI accessible to non-technical professionals. Those who can leverage these tools will have a significant advantage in nearly any career.

2. **Enhanced Productivity**: Studies show that professionals who effectively use AI tools can be twice as productive as those who don't, completing tasks faster and with better results.

3. **Problem-Solving Power**: AI provides powerful ways to analyze information, identify patterns, and generate creative solutions that might not be obvious to the human mind.

4. **Competitive Advantage**: Whether you're a small business owner, a freelancer, or an employee, understanding how to leverage AI gives you capabilities that were previously only available to large organizations with technical teams.

5. **Future-Proofing Your Career**: As AI continues to automate routine tasks, the most valuable skills will be those that complement AI – creativity, critical thinking, and the ability to effectively use AI tools to enhance your work.

What Makes This Book Different

Unlike most AI resources that are written for technical audiences, this book takes a completely different approach:

- **No Coding Required**: Everything you'll learn can be accomplished with user-friendly, no-code tools that anyone can master.

- **Practical Over Theoretical**: Instead of deep dives into how machine learning algorithms work, we focus on practical applications that deliver immediate value.

- **Visual Learning**: Descriptions of step-by-step processes make concepts easy to grasp and apply.

- **Real-World Applications**: Every concept is connected to real-world scenarios you can use in your personal or professional life.

- **Ethical Considerations**: We address the responsible use of AI throughout, ensuring you understand not just how to use these powerful tools, but when and why to use them.

How to Use This Book

This book is structured as a 7-day learning journey, with each day building upon the previous one. Here's how to get the most out of it:

6. **Follow the Sequence**: While you might be tempted to jump to specific sections, the concepts build on each other, so following the sequence will give you the best understanding.

7. **Complete the Practical Activities**: At the end of each day, you'll find hands-on activities that reinforce the concepts you've learned. Don't skip these – they're essential for truly mastering the material.

8. **Explore the Recommended Tools**: We've carefully selected tools that are user-friendly, powerful, and mostly free or offering free trials. Create accounts and familiarize yourself with them as you go.

9. **Take Notes**: Keep track of ideas for how you might apply AI in your specific situation. These personal connections will help the material stick.

10. **Be Patient**: Some concepts might seem challenging at first, but remember – millions of non-technical people are successfully using these tools every day. If they can do it, so can you!

A Note on AI Ethics

As we explore the power of AI throughout this book, we'll consistently highlight ethical considerations. AI is a powerful tool, but like any tool, it must be used responsibly. We'll discuss issues like bias, privacy, security, and the importance of maintaining human oversight in AI-assisted processes.

Let's Begin Your AI Journey

By the end of this 7-day journey, you'll have the practical skills to leverage AI in your daily life and work. You'll understand the capabilities and limitations of today's AI tools, and you'll be equipped to stay ahead of the curve as AI continues to evolve.

Are you ready to become AI-capable without writing a single line of code? Then turn the page, and let's begin Day 1 of your AI mastery journey.

Welcome to Day 1 of your journey to AI mastery! Today, we'll build a solid foundation by exploring what artificial intelligence really is, how it works in simple terms, and how it's already affecting your daily life – often in ways you might not even realize.

What AI Really Is (and Isn't)

Let's start by clearing up some common misconceptions about AI:

What AI Is:
- AI is a set of technologies that enable computers to perform tasks that typically require human intelligence
- AI is a tool created by humans to solve specific problems
- AI systems learn from data and improve their performance over time
- AI excels at finding patterns in large amounts of information

What AI Is Not:
- AI is not sentient or conscious like humans (despite what science fiction might suggest)
- AI doesn't "think" or "understand" in the human sense
- AI is not a magical solution that can solve any problem perfectly
- AI is not destined to replace humans, but rather to complement human capabilities

At its core, artificial intelligence is about creating systems that can process information, learn from it, and make decisions or predictions based on what they've learned. The key difference between AI and traditional software is that AI can improve its performance without explicit programming for every possible scenario.

Types of AI: Narrow vs. General Intelligence

When discussing AI, it's important to understand that there are different types and capabilities:

Narrow AI (or Weak AI):
- Designed for a specific task or domain
- Examples include voice assistants, recommendation systems, and image recognition
- This is the type of AI that exists today and that we'll focus on in this book
- While impressive at specific tasks, narrow AI has no general intelligence or awareness

General AI (or Strong AI):
- Would possess human-like intelligence across a wide range of tasks
- Could transfer learning from one domain to another without specific training
- Does not currently exist and may be decades away from reality
- Remains largely in the realm of science fiction

The AI tools we'll explore in this book are all examples of narrow AI – they're very good at specific tasks but don't possess general intelligence. Understanding this distinction helps set realistic expectations about what AI can and cannot do.

How AI Works: A Non-Technical Explanation

Let's demystify how AI actually works, without getting into complex mathematics or programming concepts:

The Learning Process

AI systems learn much like humans do – through experience, but at a much larger scale:

11. **Data Collection**: AI systems are fed large amounts of examples (data) related to the task they need to perform.

12. **Pattern Recognition**: The system analyzes this data to identify patterns and relationships.

13. **Model Building**: These patterns are used to create a "model" – essentially a set of rules or connections that help the system make decisions.

14. **Testing and Refinement**: The model is tested against new data to see how well it performs, and then refined to improve accuracy.

15. **Deployment**: Once the model performs well enough, it's put to work on real tasks.

A Simple Analogy

Think of teaching a child to recognize animals:

- You show them many pictures of dogs and cats
- They begin to notice patterns (dogs have certain features, cats have others)
- They build a mental model of what makes a dog a dog and a cat a cat
- When shown a new animal, they use this model to decide whether it's a dog or cat
- If they make a mistake, you correct them, and they refine their model

AI works similarly, but with much more data and mathematical processes instead of a brain. The key difference is scale – an AI might learn from millions of examples, far more than any human could process.

Common AI Terms Explained Simply

The field of AI has its own vocabulary, but you don't need to be intimidated by it. Here are some key terms explained in plain language:

Machine Learning: The process by which computers learn from data without being explicitly programmed for every scenario. It's the most common approach to creating AI today.

Algorithm: A set of rules or steps that the computer follows to solve a problem or complete a task.

Training Data: The information used to teach the AI system. The quality and diversity of this data greatly affects how well the AI performs.

Model: The result of training an AI system – it's what the system uses to make predictions or decisions when given new information.

Neural Network: A type of machine learning inspired by how brain cells (neurons) connect and communicate. Particularly useful for complex tasks like image recognition.

Deep Learning: A subset of machine learning that uses neural networks with many layers (hence "deep") to learn from vast amounts of data.

Natural Language Processing (NLP): AI techniques that help computers understand, interpret, and generate human language.

Computer Vision: AI techniques that allow computers to "see" and interpret visual information from the world.

Don't worry about memorizing these terms – we'll revisit them in context throughout the book. The important thing is to understand the basic concepts.

AI in Your Everyday Life (Without You Knowing It)

You might be surprised to learn how much AI is already integrated into your daily activities. Here are some ways AI is likely part of your life right now:

Entertainment:
- Streaming services like Netflix use AI to recommend shows and movies

- Music apps like Spotify create personalized playlists based on your listening habits
- Social media feeds are curated by AI to show content you're likely to engage with

Communication:
- Email services filter spam and categorize messages using AI
- Predictive text suggests words as you type messages
- Voice assistants like Siri and Alexa use AI to understand and respond to commands

Shopping:
- Online retailers recommend products based on your browsing and purchase history
- Price optimization systems adjust costs based on demand and other factors
- Customer service chatbots help answer questions and resolve issues

Personal Finance:
- Fraud detection systems monitor your credit card for suspicious activity
- Banking apps categorize your spending using AI
- Loan applications are often evaluated using AI-powered risk assessment

Health and Wellness:
- Fitness trackers use AI to analyze your activity and sleep patterns
- Health apps might provide personalized recommendations based on your data
- Medical research is accelerated by AI analysis of patient data and scientific literature

In each of these examples, AI is working behind the scenes to process data, identify patterns, and deliver personalized experiences or improved efficiency. As we progress through this book, you'll learn how to harness similar capabilities for your own purposes.

Practical Activity: Your First AI Interaction

Now that we've explored the basics, let's get hands-on with a simple activity to experience AI firsthand. For this exercise, we'll use one of the most accessible AI tools available today – a large language model chatbot.

Activity: Have a Conversation with an AI Assistant

16. Open your web browser and go to chat.openai.com (ChatGPT) or claude.ai (Claude) to access a free AI assistant. Both offer free versions that are powerful enough for our purposes. Create an account if you don't already have one.

17. Start a new conversation and try asking the AI these questions to explore its capabilities:
    - "Can you explain what artificial intelligence is to a 10-year-old?"
    - "Write a short poem about learning new technology."
    - "What are three ways AI might help someone in [your profession or hobby]?"
    - "Summarize the main advantages and limitations of today's AI technology."

18. Notice how the AI responds to different types of requests – factual questions, creative tasks, personalized advice, and analytical thinking.

19. Try to "stress test" the AI by asking it something very specific to your interests or industry. How well does it handle specialized knowledge?

20. Ask the AI to explain something you don't understand. Then ask it to explain the same concept in a different way if the first explanation wasn't clear.

Reflection Questions:

After completing this activity, take a few minutes to reflect on these questions:

- What impressed you about the AI's responses?
- What limitations did you notice?
- How might this type of AI assist you in your daily life or work?
- What ethical concerns might arise from using this technology?

Write down your thoughts – they'll be valuable as we continue our journey through more sophisticated AI applications in the coming days.

Day 1 Summary

Today, we've laid the groundwork for your AI journey by exploring:
- What AI truly is and isn't, beyond the hype and science fiction
- The difference between narrow and general AI
- How AI systems learn and make decisions in simple terms
- Common terminology that will help you navigate the AI landscape
- How AI is already integrated into your everyday experiences
- A hands-on activity to experience conversational AI firsthand

You've taken the first important step toward AI mastery by understanding the fundamentals. These concepts will serve as building blocks as we move forward to explore specific tools and applications.

Tomorrow's Preview: On Day 2, we'll dive into the exciting world of no-code AI tools that allow anyone to create AI applications without programming. You'll discover how the democratization of AI technology is putting powerful capabilities in the hands of non-technical users like yourself. We'll explore user-friendly platforms and set up your personal AI toolkit with free options that deliver impressive results.

Rest up, and get ready for a hands-on day of discovery tomorrow!

Welcome to Day 2 of your AI mastery journey! Yesterday, we built a foundation by understanding what AI is and how it works in simple terms. Today, we're taking an exciting step forward by exploring the world of no-code AI tools – platforms that allow anyone to harness the power of artificial intelligence without writing a single line of code.

The Rise of No-Code AI Platforms

One of the most significant developments in recent years has been the democratization of AI through no-code platforms. These tools have transformed AI from a technology only accessible to specialized engineers into something anyone can use.

From Coding to Clicking

Traditionally, implementing AI solutions required:
- Expertise in programming languages like Python
- Understanding of complex mathematical concepts
- Knowledge of specialized AI frameworks
- Months or years of technical education

Today's no-code AI platforms have changed the game by:
- Providing visual interfaces for building AI solutions
- Handling the technical complexity behind the scenes
- Offering pre-built models for common tasks
- Making AI accessible through simple drag-and-drop interfaces

According to industry research, by 2024, low-code and no-code application development will be responsible for more than 65% of application development activity. This shift isn't just making technology more accessible – it's transforming how businesses operate and how individuals solve problems.

Why This Matters to You

The rise of no-code AI means that you don't need to be a technical specialist to:
- Analyze large datasets for insights
- Automate repetitive tasks
- Create intelligent systems that learn from experience
- Keep pace with technological change in your industry

No-code platforms have effectively removed the technical barrier to entry, allowing you to focus on applying AI to solve real problems rather than struggling with implementation details.

Top Beginner-Friendly AI Tools in 2025

Let's explore some of the most user-friendly and powerful no-code AI tools available today. Each of these platforms offers free tiers or trials that make them perfect for beginners:

1. ChatGPT and Claude (Conversational AI)

What they do: These large language models can understand and generate human-like text, allowing you to have conversations, draft content, brainstorm ideas, analyze information, and much more.

Best for: Writing, research, creative ideation, learning, and simple problem-solving.

Getting started: Both offer free tiers that give you access to powerful AI capabilities through a simple chat interface.

2. Microsoft Lobe (Computer Vision)

What it does: Allows you to create custom image recognition models by simply providing example images.

Best for: Building systems that can identify objects, categorize images, or detect visual patterns.

Getting started: Download the free application, create a project, and start labeling images to train your model.

3. Akkio (Predictive Analytics)

What it does: Enables you to make predictions based on data without complex data science.

Best for: Sales forecasting, customer churn prediction, lead scoring, and other business analytics.

Getting started: Upload a spreadsheet, select what you want to predict, and the platform builds a custom AI model for you.

4. Canva Magic Studio (AI-Powered Design)

What it does: Uses AI to help create professional designs, edit images, generate visuals from text descriptions, and more.

Best for: Creating marketing materials, presentations, social media content, and other visual assets.

Getting started: Sign up for a free account and explore the AI-powered features within the familiar design interface.

5. Synthesia (Video Creation)

What it does: Allows you to create professional videos with AI-generated presenters speaking your script in multiple languages.

Best for: Training videos, product demos, marketing content, and multilingual communication.

Getting started: Create a free account to explore the platform and see how AI can turn text into engaging video content.

6. RunwayML (Creative Media Tools)

What it does: Offers a suite of AI tools for video editing, image generation, and creative projects.

Best for: Content creators, artists, and anyone looking to enhance visual media with AI.

Getting started: Sign up for a free account and experiment with their various creative AI tools.

7. Midjourney (Image Generation)

What it does: Creates stunning, high-quality images based on text descriptions.

Best for: Generating custom illustrations, concept art, and visual assets for various projects.

Getting started: Join their Discord server and use the free trial to generate your first AI-created images.

8. Otter.ai (Audio Transcription and Analysis)

What it does: Automatically transcribes and analyzes conversations, meetings, and audio content.

Best for: Meeting notes, interview transcription, content repurposing, and research.

Getting started: Sign up for a free account and start transcribing your first audio file or live conversation.

These tools represent just a small sample of what's available. As you continue your AI journey, you'll discover many more specialized platforms that address specific needs. The key is to start with tools that align with your interests and practical needs.

Setting Up Your AI Toolkit (All Free Options)

Now, let's set up your personal AI toolkit with a selection of free tools that will give you a powerful starting point for exploring AI applications:

Step 1: Create Accounts for Essential AI Services

Let's start by setting up accounts for these core services:

21. **ChatGPT (chat.openai.com)** or **Claude (claude.ai)**
    - Sign up for a free account
    - Note that ChatGPT's free tier uses GPT-3.5, while paid users get access to GPT-4

22. **Canva (canva.com)**
    - Create a free account
    - Explore the Magic Studio features for AI-powered design

23. **Midjourney (via Discord)**
    - Create a Discord account if you don't have one
    - Join the Midjourney server and set up your free trial

Step 2: Download Desktop Applications

Some no-code AI tools work best as desktop applications:

24. **Microsoft Lobe (lobe.ai)**
    - Download the free application for your operating system
    - Install and create your first project folder

Step 3: Organize Your AI Workspace

To make the most of your new tools:

25. **Create a dedicated folder** on your computer for AI projects
26. **Bookmark the web-based tools** in a specific folder in your browser
27. **Prepare sample data** you might want to use (images, text, spreadsheets)

Step 4: Set Up Cloud Storage

Many AI tools work with files you'll want to access across devices:

28. Sign up for a free cloud storage service if you don't already use one (Google Drive, Dropbox, or OneDrive)
29. Create a specific folder for your AI projects and materials

By completing these steps, you'll have a complete AI toolkit ready for exploration and practical application. These tools collectively give you capabilities that would have required extensive technical expertise just a few years ago.

Understanding AI Models Without the Math

Before we dive into creating your first AI project, let's briefly demystify what's happening behind the scenes when you use these no-code tools.

What Is an AI Model?

At the heart of every AI tool is something called a "model." You can think of an AI model as a recipe that the computer follows to make decisions or predictions based on new information.

Models are created through a process called "training," where the AI system learns from examples. There are several types of models, each suited to different tasks:

Classification Models: Categorize things into groups (Is this email spam or not? Is this image a cat or a dog?)

Regression Models: Predict numerical values (What will this house sell for? How many units will we sell next month?)

Generative Models: Create new content similar to what they've learned from (Write a poem about nature. Create an image of a futuristic city.)

Recommendation Models: Suggest items or actions based on patterns (You might like this movie. This product would interest you.)

The beauty of no-code platforms is that they handle all the complex mathematics and programming involved in creating these models. You just need to provide the examples and specify what you want the model to do.

Pre-trained vs. Custom Models

When using no-code AI tools, you'll encounter two approaches:

Pre-trained Models: These are already trained on massive datasets and ready to use. Tools like ChatGPT, Claude, and Midjourney use pre-trained models that you can immediately apply to various tasks.

Custom Models: Some platforms allow you to create your own specialized models by providing examples relevant to your specific needs. Microsoft Lobe and Akkio fall into this category.

Understanding this distinction helps you choose the right approach for different situations:

- Use pre-trained models when you need general capabilities or when you don't have specific data
- Create custom models when you have unique requirements or specialized data that general models might not understand

Practical Activity: Create Your First AI Project

Now it's time to put your new knowledge into action by creating your first AI project. For this activity, we'll use Microsoft Lobe to build an image recognition system – no coding required!

Project: Building an Image Classifier

What you'll need:
- Microsoft Lobe installed on your computer
- A collection of at least 20 images divided into 2-3 categories (e.g., different types of plants, food items, or household objects)

Step 1: Set Up Your Project
30. Open Microsoft Lobe
31. Create a new project and give it a meaningful name
32. Decide what categories you want your model to recognize

Step 2: Import and Label Your Images
33. Click the "Import" button to add images to your project
34. Assign each image to the appropriate category (label)
35. Continue adding images until you have at least 5-10 examples per category

Step 3: Train Your Model
36. Once you've imported and labeled your images, Lobe will automatically begin training your model
37. Watch as the training progress indicator shows the model learning from your examples
38. The more diverse and numerous your examples, the better your model will perform

Step 4: Test Your Model

39. Use the "Use" tab to test your model with new images
40. Try images similar to but different from your training examples
41. Notice how the model predicts the category and shows its confidence level

Step 5: Improve Your Model

42. If your model makes mistakes, correct them by adding the misclassified image to your dataset with the proper label
43. Add more diverse examples to categories where the model performs poorly
44. Notice how the model improves as you provide more guidance

Reflection Questions:

- How accurate was your model's classification?
- What factors seemed to affect its performance?
- What practical applications can you imagine for this type of AI?
- How does building this model help you understand how AI learns?

This simple project demonstrates the core principle behind many AI applications: learning from examples. The more quality examples you provide, the better the AI performs. And you've accomplished this without writing a single line of code!

Day 2 Summary

Today, we've taken a major step in your AI journey by:

- Understanding how no-code platforms are democratizing AI technology
- Exploring top beginner-friendly AI tools available in 2024
- Setting up your personal AI toolkit with free resources

- Learning about AI models without getting lost in technical details
- Creating your first custom AI project using Microsoft Lobe

You've now experienced firsthand how accessible AI has become. The platforms we've explored today will serve as your gateway to more sophisticated applications as your skills develop.

Tomorrow's Preview: On Day 3, we'll delve into the exciting world of generative AI, exploring how to create professional-quality text, images, videos, and audio using AI tools. You'll learn how to leverage these capabilities for personal projects, professional work, and creative endeavors.

Great job today! You're well on your way to becoming AI-capable without any coding required.

Welcome to Day 3 of your AI mastery journey! Yesterday, we explored the world of no-code AI tools and even created your first AI project. Today, we're diving into one of the most exciting areas of AI technology: generative AI. These powerful tools can create new content – text, images, videos, and audio – that appears to be made by humans. By the end of today, you'll be able to leverage these capabilities to produce professional-quality content for a variety of purposes.

Text Generation: Writing with AI Assistants

Let's start with text generation, which has become incredibly sophisticated in recent years thanks to large language models (LLMs) like ChatGPT, Claude, and Gemini.

How AI Text Generation Works

At a high level, these systems:
45. Are trained on billions of text examples from books, articles, websites, and other sources
46. Learn patterns and relationships between words, concepts, and ideas
47. Generate new text by predicting what words should come next in a sequence
48. Can be guided by your prompts and instructions to create specific types of content

The key to using these tools effectively is understanding how to craft prompts that guide the AI toward your desired outcome.

The Art of Prompt Engineering

Prompt engineering is the skill of crafting inputs that elicit the best possible outputs from AI systems. Here are some fundamental techniques:

Be Specific and Detailed:
- Bad prompt: "Write about dogs."
- Good prompt: "Write a 300-word informative article about the health benefits of owning dogs, including both physical and mental health aspects. Include 3-4 scientific facts with explanations."

Specify Format and Style:
- Bad prompt: "Write marketing copy."
- Good prompt: "Write Facebook ad copy for a new organic skincare line targeting women aged 25-40. Use a friendly,

conversational tone. The copy should be 50-75 words and emphasize natural ingredients and sustainability."

Use Role Prompting:
- Bad prompt: "Help me write a legal document."
- Good prompt: "Acting as an experienced contract lawyer, help me draft a simple non-disclosure agreement between a freelance designer and a small business. Use plain language where possible."

Iterate and Refine:
Start with a basic output, then ask the AI to improve specific aspects:
- "Please rewrite this to make it more concise."
- "Can you adjust the tone to be more professional?"
- "Add more technical details to the third paragraph."

Practical Applications for AI Writing

Here are some of the most useful ways to apply AI text generation:

Content Creation:
- Blog posts and articles
- Social media content
- Email newsletters
- Website copy

Business Communication:
- Email drafting and responses
- Meeting summaries
- Internal documentation
- Client proposals

Creative Writing:
- Story ideas and outlines
- Character development
- Dialogue generation
- Poetry and creative prompts

Research and Learning:
- Summarizing complex topics
- Explaining difficult concepts
- Creating study guides
- Generating practice questions

Personal Productivity:
- Drafting personal emails
- Creating to-do lists
- Planning events
- Brainstorming ideas

Ethical Considerations in AI Writing

As you explore these powerful tools, keep these ethical principles in mind:

Transparency: Be honest about using AI assistance when appropriate, especially in professional contexts.

Accuracy Verification: Always fact-check AI-generated content, as these systems can confidently present incorrect information.

Avoiding Misrepresentation: Don't use AI to create false testimonials, reviews, or to impersonate real people.

Respecting Intellectual Property: Understand that AI-generated content based on copyrighted material raises complex legal and ethical questions.

Image Creation: Designing Without Design Skills

AI image generation has made remarkable progress in recent years. Tools like DALL-E, Midjourney, and Stable Diffusion can create stunning visuals from text descriptions, opening up creative possibilities for people with no traditional design skills.

How AI Image Generation Works

These systems:
49. Are trained on millions of image-text pairs
50. Learn to associate visual elements with words and concepts
51. Generate new images based on text prompts
52. Continue to improve as they receive feedback

Crafting Effective Image Prompts

Creating great AI-generated images is all about the prompt. Here are some techniques for better results:

Be Descriptive and Specific:
• Basic prompt: "A house in the mountains."

- Improved prompt: "A cozy wooden cabin in snow-covered mountains at sunset, with warm light glowing from windows, pine trees in foreground, professional photography, sharp focus."

Specify Artistic Style:
- "A portrait of a young woman in the style of Rembrandt, dramatic lighting, oil painting."
- "A futuristic city skyline in cyberpunk style, neon colors, digital art, 8K resolution."

Include Technical Parameters:
- "Ultra-detailed, realistic texture, cinematic lighting, 8K UHD, ray tracing."
- "Isometric view, soft colors, minimalist design, clean background."

Use Negative Prompts:
Some tools allow you to specify what you don't want in the image:
- "No blurry elements, no distorted faces, no text, no watermarks."

Practical Applications for AI Image Generation

Here are valuable ways to use AI image generation:

Marketing and Branding:
- Social media graphics
- Blog post illustrations
- Product mockups
- Banner ads

Presentations and Documents:
- Custom slides and backgrounds

- Report illustrations
- Infographic elements
- Visual metaphors for concepts

Personal Projects:
- Custom artwork for your home
- Personalized greeting cards
- Social media profile images
- Vision boards

Creative Exploration:
- Concept art for stories or games
- Visualizing ideas before creation
- Exploring visual styles
- Artistic experimentation

Ethical Considerations in AI Image Creation

As with text generation, there are important ethical aspects to consider:

Image Rights: Understand that the legal status of AI-generated images is still evolving.

Avoiding Harmful Content: Don't use these tools to create deceptive, harmful, or inappropriate images.

Cultural Sensitivity: Be aware that AI systems may reflect cultural biases in how they generate certain imagery.

Originality vs. Derivation: Recognize that AI images are derived from existing works and consider this when using them commercially.

Video Production: From Text to Moving Images

AI video generation is one of the newest frontiers in generative AI. While still evolving, today's tools offer impressive capabilities for creating video content without traditional production methods.

Current AI Video Capabilities

Today's AI video tools generally fall into these categories:

Text-to-Video Generation:
- Create short video clips from text descriptions
- Examples: Runway Gen-2, HeyGen, Synthesia

Avatar-Based Video:
- Generate videos with AI presenters speaking your script
- Examples: Synthesia, D-ID, HeyGen

Video Editing and Enhancement:
- Automatically edit footage, remove backgrounds, or enhance quality
- Examples: Runway, Descript, Opus Clip

Animation and Motion Graphics:
- Convert static images to animated sequences
- Examples: RunwayML, Lumen5, Pictory

Getting Started with AI Video

For beginners, avatar-based video platforms offer the easiest entry point:

Using Synthesia for Your First AI Video:

53. Sign up for a Synthesia account (free trial available)
54. Select an AI avatar from their library
55. Enter your script text
56. Choose voice, language, and background
57. Generate your video
58. Review and make adjustments as needed

These simple steps produce a professional-looking video with an AI presenter delivering your message – no camera, microphone, or video editing skills required.

Practical Applications for AI Video

Consider these valuable use cases:

Business Communication:
- Training videos
- Product demonstrations
- Company announcements
- Client presentations

Education:
- Instructional content
- Explainer videos
- Multi-language tutorials

- Lecture summaries

Marketing:
- Social media content
- Product introductions
- Customer testimonials (using your script)
- Event promotions

Personal Projects:
- Video greetings
- Social media content
- Narrated photo collections
- Multilingual messaging

Ethical Considerations in AI Video

AI video raises unique ethical questions:

Representation and Consent: Consider whether using an AI avatar of a certain demographic is appropriate for your message.

Transparency: Always be clear when video content is AI-generated, especially in business contexts.

Potential for Misuse: Be aware of the potential for deepfakes and misrepresentation, and use these tools responsibly.

Voice Rights: When using AI voices based on real people, ensure you're using properly licensed voices with appropriate permissions.

Audio Generation: Creating Voice and Music

AI audio generation includes both speech synthesis (text-to-speech) and music creation. These tools allow you to produce audio content without recording equipment or musical expertise.

AI Voice Generation

Modern AI voice tools have become remarkably natural-sounding:

Key Capabilities:
- Convert text to lifelike speech
- Offer multiple languages and accents
- Control tone, pace, and emphasis
- Create consistent voice identity

Leading Tools:
- ElevenLabs
- Murf.ai
- Play.ht
- NaturalReader

Getting Started with ElevenLabs:
59. Create an account (free tier available)
60. Enter your text
61. Select from available voices
62. Adjust settings (speed, stability, clarity)
63. Generate and download your audio

The quality of today's AI voices is so good that they're being used for audiobooks, podcasts, and professional narration.

AI Music Generation

AI music creation has also made significant advances:

Key Capabilities:
- Generate original music in various genres
- Create background tracks for videos
- Produce mood-based instrumentals
- Customize duration and structure

Leading Tools:
- Suno
- AIVA
- Soundraw
- Mubert

Getting Started with Suno:
64. Sign up for an account
65. Describe the type of music you want
66. Specify genre, mood, and instruments
67. Generate your track
68. Download or refine the result

These tools make custom music creation accessible to anyone, regardless of musical ability.

Practical Applications for AI Audio

Consider these valuable use cases:

Voice Applications:
- Podcast narration
- Video voiceovers
- Audiobook production
- Multilingual content

Music Applications:
- Video background music
- Podcast intros and transitions
- Social media content
- Presentation backgrounds

Combined Applications:
- Complete podcast episodes
- Audio advertisements
- Guided meditations
- Educational content

Ethical Considerations in AI Audio

As with other generative AI, there are important ethical aspects to consider:

Voice Cloning Concerns: Be careful about creating voice content that could be mistaken for a real person.

Music Copyright: Understand the terms of use for AI-generated music, especially for commercial applications.

Disclosure: Be transparent about using AI-generated audio in professional contexts.

Cultural Sensitivity: Be mindful of how you represent different accents and musical traditions.

Ethical Considerations in AI Creation

Throughout this chapter, we've touched on various ethical considerations for different types of generative AI. Let's explore some overarching principles that apply across all generative AI tools:

Transparency and Honesty

Always be upfront about using AI-generated content. This is especially important in:

- Professional contexts
- Academic settings
- Journalistic content
- Marketing materials

In some cases, disclosure might be a legal requirement, but even when it's not, transparency builds trust.

Quality and Accuracy Control

AI-generated content requires human oversight:

- Fact-check information before sharing
- Review for unintended biases or problematic content
- Ensure the tone and style are appropriate
- Verify that the content meets your quality standards

Remember that while AI can produce impressive content, you are responsible for what you choose to publish or share.

Respect for Intellectual Property

The legal landscape around AI-created content is still evolving:
- Understand the terms of service for the AI tools you use
- Be aware that some AI systems are trained on copyrighted material
- Consider whether you have the right to use AI-generated content commercially
- When in doubt, consult with a legal professional

Preventing Harmful Uses

Commit to using generative AI responsibly:
- Don't create misleading or deceptive content
- Avoid generating content that could harm individuals or groups
- Be mindful of privacy concerns when creating realistic images of people
- Consider the potential consequences of your creations

Human Creativity and AI Collaboration

Think of AI as a collaborator rather than a replacement:
- Use AI to enhance your creative process, not replace it
- Bring your unique human perspective to AI-generated content
- Iterate and refine AI outputs to align with your vision
- Recognize the complementary strengths of human and AI creation

Practical Activity: Generate Professional Content

Now it's time to put your new knowledge into practice by creating a multi-modal content package using several generative AI tools. This activity will help you understand how different AI tools can work together to produce a cohesive set of professional content.

Project: Create a Mini Content Campaign

What you'll create:
- A short informational article (text)
- A featured image (image)
- A 30-second promotional video (video)
- A voice narration of key points (audio)

Topic Options: Choose one of these topics or create your own:
- "5 Ways to Improve Productivity While Working from Home"
- "Understanding the Basics of Personal Finance"
- "Beginner's Guide to Sustainable Living"
- "Essential Tips for Digital Wellness"

Step 1: Generate the Article
69. Using ChatGPT or Claude, create a 300-400 word article on your chosen topic
70. Prompt: "Write a 300-400 word informative article about [your topic]. Include an engaging introduction, 3-5 main points with brief explanations, and a conclusion. Use a conversational, friendly tone that's accessible to beginners."
71. Review and refine the output until you're satisfied

Step 2: Create a Featured Image

72. Using Midjourney or DALL-E, generate an image that represents your topic
73. Prompt: "Create a professional featured image for an article about [your topic]. The image should be clean, modern, and suitable for a blog or social media. Include relevant visual elements like [specific elements related to your topic]."
74. Generate several options and select your favorite

Step 3: Produce a Short Video

75. Using Synthesia or a similar platform, create a 30-second video
76. Write a script that highlights the key points from your article
77. Select an avatar, background, and voice that matches your content's tone
78. Generate the video and review it

Step 4: Create an Audio Narration

79. Using ElevenLabs or another text-to-speech tool, create an audio version
80. Extract the most important 100-150 words from your article
81. Generate the audio narration
82. Review for natural pacing and pronunciation

Step 5: Combine and Reflect

83. Imagine how these elements could work together in a real campaign
84. Consider how you might use each element on different platforms
85. Reflect on the quality, consistency, and cohesiveness of your AI-generated content

Reflection Questions:

- How does the quality of the AI-generated content compare to what you could create without AI?

- What aspects required the most human intervention or refinement?
- How might you use similar AI-generated content in your personal or professional life?
- What ethical considerations arose during this process?

By completing this activity, you've experienced the full range of generative AI capabilities across multiple modalities. This integrated approach shows how powerful these tools can be when used together.

Day 3 Summary

Today, we've explored the exciting world of generative AI across multiple formats:
- Text generation with large language models and effective prompt engineering
- Image creation using text-to-image systems and prompt optimization
- Video production with avatar-based platforms and text-to-video tools
- Audio generation for both voice content and music
- Ethical considerations across all types of AI-generated content
- A hands-on project creating a multi-modal content package

You've now experienced firsthand how these technologies can help you create professional-quality content without specialized skills in writing, design, video production, or audio engineering.

Tomorrow's Preview: On Day 4, we'll focus on boosting your productivity with AI. You'll learn how to automate routine tasks, streamline your workflow, and use AI for research, document analysis, and personal organization. These practical applications will help you save time and increase efficiency in both your personal and professional life.

Great work today! You're making excellent progress on your AI mastery journey.

Welcome to Day 5 of your AI mastery journey! Yesterday, we explored how AI can boost your productivity through automation and workflow enhancements. Today, we're focusing on perhaps the most valuable application of AI for non-technical users: using AI to make better decisions. By the end of today, you'll understand how to leverage AI tools to analyze data, gather insights, and make more informed choices – all without needing a background in data science.

Understanding Data Without Being a Data Scientist

Data has become essential for decision-making in business and personal contexts alike. However, the skills needed to analyze data effectively have traditionally required specialized training. AI is changing that dynamic.

How AI Democratizes Data Analysis

AI tools are making data analysis accessible to everyone through:

Natural Language Interfaces:
- Ask questions about your data in plain English

- No need to know programming or query languages
- Get answers in understandable, conversational responses

Automated Pattern Recognition:
- AI identifies trends and correlations automatically
- It highlights anomalies and points of interest
- It can discover insights that might otherwise be missed

Visual Data Exploration:
- AI can generate and explain data visualizations
- It can recommend appropriate chart types for different data
- It can interpret what visualizations mean in practical terms

From Raw Data to Actionable Insights

The process of turning data into decisions typically follows this path:

86. **Data Collection** - Gathering relevant information
87. **Data Preparation** - Cleaning and organizing the information
88. **Analysis** - Identifying patterns and relationships
89. **Insight Generation** - Extracting meaningful findings
90. **Decision Support** - Using findings to inform choices

Traditionally, steps 2-4 required technical expertise. AI now assists with all these steps, allowing non-technical users to move directly from having data to making decisions.

Practical No-Code Data Analysis

Here are some ways to analyze data without technical skills:

Using ChatGPT or Claude for Data Analysis:

91. For Spreadsheet Data:
- Copy data from your spreadsheet
- Paste it into ChatGPT or Claude
- Ask: "Analyze this data and tell me the key trends and insights"
- Follow up with specific questions about patterns or relationships

92. For Text-Based Information:
- Input text-based data (survey responses, reviews, etc.)
- Ask: "Summarize the main themes in this text data"
- Request categorization of responses into relevant groups
- Ask for identification of sentiment or emotional tone

93. For Numerical Analysis:
- Share numerical data points and ask for statistical analysis
- Request comparisons between different time periods or categories
- Ask for projections based on historical patterns
- Inquire about potential correlations between different variables

Using Specialized No-Code Tools:

Tools like Obviously AI, MonkeyLearn, and Akkio allow you to:
- Upload data through simple interfaces
- Select what you want to analyze or predict
- Get results through visual dashboards
- Explore "what-if" scenarios without coding

· Using AI for Market Research

Market research has traditionally been expensive and time-consuming. AI tools are making it more accessible and affordable for everyone from small business owners to product managers.

AI-Powered Market Intelligence

AI can help you gather and analyze market information in several ways:

Trend Identification:
- Track emerging topics and conversations across the web
- Identify growing interest in specific products or services
- Spot shifts in consumer preferences and behaviors

Competitive Analysis:
- Monitor competitor activities, pricing, and positioning
- Analyze competitor strengths and vulnerabilities
- Identify gaps and opportunities in the market

Audience Insights:
- Analyze demographic and psychographic data
- Uncover audience needs, preferences, and pain points
- Identify potential target segments and their characteristics

Practical Market Research Techniques

Here's how to leverage AI for effective market research:

1. Trend Analysis with AI:

To identify emerging trends:

94. Use AI-powered search tools like Perplexity.ai or Google Trends
95. Ask: "What are the emerging trends in [your industry] in 2024?"
96. Follow up with: "Which of these trends is growing fastest and why?"
97. Request evidence and sources to validate the trends

2. Competitive Landscape Mapping:

To understand your competitive environment:

98. List your known competitors for your AI assistant
99. Ask: "Who are other significant competitors in this space I might have missed?"
100. Request a comparison of features, pricing, and positioning
101. Ask for identification of each competitor's unique selling proposition

3. Target Audience Analysis:

To better understand potential customers:

102. Provide your AI assistant with any customer data you have
103. Ask: "Based on this information, what are the key characteristics of my ideal customer?"
104. Request a segmentation of your audience into distinct groups
105. Ask for recommendations on how to appeal to each segment

Tools for AI-Enhanced Market Research

Several specialized tools can enhance your market research:

Social Listening Platforms:

- Tools like Brandwatch and Mention use AI to analyze social media conversations
- They track brand mentions, sentiment, and trending topics
- They provide insights into how your brand or industry is perceived

Review Analysis Tools:
- AI can analyze product reviews across multiple platforms
- It can identify common praise points and complaints
- It can track sentiment changes over time or after specific events

Survey and Feedback Analysis:
- AI tools can process open-ended survey responses
- They can categorize feedback into themes and sentiment
- They can highlight actionable insights from customer feedback

Customer Insights Through AI Analysis

Understanding customer behavior and preferences is critical for business success. AI offers powerful ways to gain deeper customer insights without complex analysis.

From Customer Data to Customer Understanding

AI helps transform raw customer data into meaningful insights:

Behavioral Pattern Recognition:
- Identify common customer journeys and interaction patterns
- Spot bottlenecks or drop-off points in the customer experience
- Recognize triggers for purchases or engagement

Segmentation and Persona Development:

- Group customers based on behavior, preferences, and value
- Create detailed profiles of different customer segments
- Identify the unique needs and characteristics of each group

Sentiment and Satisfaction Analysis:

- Monitor customer sentiment across touchpoints
- Identify drivers of satisfaction and dissatisfaction
- Track changes in sentiment over time or across segments

Practical Customer Analysis Techniques

Here's how to use AI to better understand your customers:

1. Customer Feedback Analysis:

To make sense of customer feedback:

106. Gather feedback from reviews, surveys, support tickets, etc.
107. Input this text into your AI assistant
108. Ask: "Analyze this customer feedback and identify the main themes and sentiment"
109. Follow up with: "What specific product/service improvements would address the most common issues?"

2. Customer Segmentation:

To segment your customer base:

110. Prepare basic customer data (purchase history, demographics, behavior)
111. Share this data with your AI assistant
112. Ask: "Based on this data, what distinct customer segments can you identify?"

113.   Request characteristics and recommendations for each segment

3. Churn Risk Identification:

To predict potential customer loss:
114.   Share data about past customers who left and those who stayed
115.   Ask your AI assistant to identify patterns among those who churned
116.   Request warning signs that might indicate churn risk
117.   Ask for retention strategies tailored to at-risk customers

Voice of Customer Analysis

AI excels at processing unstructured customer feedback:

Review Mining:
- Analyze online reviews to extract specific product feedback
- Identify most-mentioned features, both positively and negatively
- Track changes in customer sentiment over time

Support Conversation Analysis:
- Process customer service interactions for insights
- Identify common questions, issues, and confusion points
- Spot opportunities for proactive communication or product improvement

Social Media Monitoring:
- Track brand mentions and discussions across platforms
- Analyze context and sentiment of conversations
- Identify potential brand advocates and detractors

Financial Planning with AI Tools

Financial decision-making often involves complex calculations and considerations. AI tools can simplify this process and provide personalized guidance.

AI-Assisted Financial Analysis

AI can help with various aspects of financial planning:

Budget Optimization:
- Analyze spending patterns to identify savings opportunities
- Recommend budget adjustments based on goals and habits
- Project the impact of different budgeting approaches

Investment Research:
- Analyze investment options based on your risk profile
- Compare historical performance across different scenarios
- Monitor news and trends that might impact investments

Financial Goal Planning:
- Calculate realistic timelines for financial goals
- Recommend saving and investment strategies
- Adjust plans based on changing circumstances

Practical Financial Planning Techniques

Here's how to use AI for better financial decision-making:

1. Personal Budget Analysis:

To optimize your personal or household budget:

118.   Gather your income and expense data for the past few months

119.   Share this information with your AI assistant

120.   Ask: "Analyze my spending patterns and suggest areas where I could save money"

121.   Request a recommended budget allocation based on standard financial principles

2. Investment Decision Support:

For investment guidance (not financial advice):

122.   Share information about your financial goals and risk tolerance

123.   Ask your AI assistant to explain different investment approaches

124.   Request an analysis of pros and cons for each approach

125.   Ask for key questions you should research before making decisions

3. Business Financial Scenario Planning:

For business financial decisions:

126.   Input your current financial data and potential scenarios

127.   Ask your AI assistant to project outcomes for different decisions

128.   Request an analysis of risk factors for each scenario

129.   Ask for key metrics you should track to evaluate success

Financial Modeling and Forecasting

AI can help create simple financial models without complex spreadsheets:

Cash Flow Projections:
- Input your expected income and expenses
- Ask the AI to create monthly cash flow projections
- Explore "what-if" scenarios with different assumptions

Return on Investment Calculations:
- Provide costs, expected returns, and timeframes
- Request ROI calculations and breakeven analysis
- Compare potential returns across different opportunities

Cost Reduction Analysis:
- Share your current cost structure
- Ask the AI to identify potential savings opportunities
- Request prioritization based on impact and feasibility

AI-Powered Forecasting for Non-Experts

Prediction and forecasting have traditionally required statistical expertise. AI now makes forecasting accessible to everyone.

From Historical Data to Future Predictions

AI can analyze patterns in historical data to project future outcomes:

Sales Forecasting:
- Predict future sales based on historical performance
- Account for seasonality and trends
- Adjust for known upcoming factors

Demand Planning:
- Project future demand for products or services
- Consider external factors like market trends
- Optimize inventory or resource allocation

Trend Projection:
- Extend current trends into future periods
- Account for acceleration or deceleration
- Identify potential turning points

Practical Forecasting Techniques

Here's how to use AI for basic forecasting without specialized skills:

1. Simple Sales Forecasting:

To project future sales:

130. Gather monthly sales data for at least the past year
131. Share this data with your AI assistant
132. Ask: "Based on this historical data, what are projected sales for the next six months?"
133. Request explanations for any seasonal patterns or trends

2. Scenario-Based Forecasting:

To understand potential future outcomes:

134. Share historical data and describe different possible scenarios
135. Ask your AI assistant to project outcomes for each scenario
136. Request a comparison of best-case, worst-case, and most likely scenarios

137. Ask for key indicators that would suggest which scenario is unfolding

3. Resource Planning Projections:

For staffing or resource allocation:

138. Share historical workload or demand data
139. Ask your AI assistant to project future resource needs
140. Request identification of potential peak periods or bottlenecks
141. Ask for recommended resource allocation strategies

Specialized Forecasting Tools

Several no-code platforms offer more sophisticated forecasting:

Time Series Forecasting Tools:
- Platforms like Akkio and Obviously AI offer time series forecasting
- They can automatically account for seasonality and trends
- They provide confidence intervals and accuracy metrics

Predictive Analytics Dashboards:
- Tools like Qlik and Tableau now include AI-powered predictive features
- They can extend visualizations into future periods
- They offer interactive "what-if" scenario planning

Industry-Specific Forecasting:
- Many industries have specialized forecasting tools
- These incorporate industry-specific factors and benchmarks
- They often include pre-built models for common forecasting needs

Practical Activity: Analyze Real Data for Actionable Insights

Now it's time to apply what you've learned by analyzing real data to extract actionable insights. This activity will help you experience the power of AI-assisted decision-making firsthand.

Project: Data-Driven Decision Analysis

What you'll need:
- A dataset relevant to your personal or professional interests
- This could be: sales data, website analytics, customer feedback, personal finances, etc.
- If you don't have data available, you can use publicly available datasets (your AI assistant can suggest sources)

Step 1: Prepare Your Data
142. Choose a dataset with information relevant to a decision you need to make
143. Organize it in a clear format (spreadsheet, text document, etc.)
144. Make note of specific questions you want answered from this data

Step 2: Initial Data Exploration
145. Share your data with ChatGPT or Claude
146. Ask: "Please analyze this data and provide a summary of the key patterns and insights"
147. Ask follow-up questions about specific aspects of the data

148.　Request visualizations the AI would recommend (which you can then create)

Step 3: Decision-Focused Analysis
149.　Explain the decision you're trying to make to your AI assistant
150.　Ask: "Based on this data, what factors should I consider in making this decision?"
151.　Request pros and cons of different potential choices
152.　Ask for data-backed recommendations

Step 4: Future Projection
153.　Ask your AI assistant to project trends based on the historical data
154.　Request best-case and worst-case scenarios
155.　Ask what additional data would strengthen the analysis
156.　Discuss how to monitor outcomes after making your decision

Step 5: Action Plan Development
157.　Based on the insights gained, ask your AI assistant to help develop an action plan
158.　Request specific, measurable steps
159.　Ask for potential obstacles and mitigation strategies
160.　Create a timeline for implementation and review

Reflection Questions:
- How did the AI-powered analysis compare to how you would have analyzed the data manually?
- What surprising insights emerged from the analysis?
- How confident do you feel in making decisions based on this analysis?
- What additional data or analysis would further improve your decision-making?

By completing this activity, you've experienced how AI can transform raw data into actionable insights without requiring technical expertise. This process can be applied to virtually any data-driven decision in your personal or professional life.

Day 5 Summary

Today, we've explored how AI can enhance your decision-making abilities:

- Understanding data without technical expertise
- Using AI for market research and competitive analysis
- Extracting customer insights from various data sources
- Leveraging AI for financial planning and analysis
- Creating forecasts and predictions without statistical knowledge
- Completing a practical activity to analyze real data for actionable insights

You now have the knowledge to make more informed decisions using AI-powered analysis, even without a background in data science or analytics.

Tomorrow's Preview: On Day 6, we'll focus on personal growth through AI. You'll discover how AI can enhance your learning, develop your skills, boost your creativity, and support your health and wellness goals. These applications will help you leverage AI for continuous personal improvement and development.

Excellent work today! You're developing a comprehensive understanding of how AI can transform various aspects of your life and work.

Welcome to Day 6 of your AI mastery journey! Yesterday, we explored how AI can enhance your decision-making by analyzing data and generating insights. Today, we're focusing on something equally valuable but perhaps more personal: using AI for your own growth and development. By the end of today, you'll understand how AI can help you learn faster, develop new skills, enhance your creativity, support your health goals, and organize your knowledge more effectively.

AI-Powered Learning Platforms

Learning has been one of the first domains to benefit significantly from AI, with personalized, adaptive learning experiences becoming increasingly accessible.

How AI Transforms Learning

AI is reshaping educational experiences through:

Personalized Learning Paths:
- Adapting content based on your knowledge level and learning style
- Identifying and addressing gaps in your understanding
- Adjusting difficulty and pacing to keep you in the optimal challenge zone

Content Enhancement:
- Summarizing complex materials into digestible formats
- Generating practice questions and exercises
- Creating visual aids and interactive elements

Progress Monitoring:

- Tracking knowledge retention over time
- Identifying areas that need reinforcement
- Predicting long-term learning outcomes

Popular AI Learning Platforms

Several platforms are leveraging AI to deliver enhanced learning experiences:

Duolingo:
- Uses AI to personalize language learning
- Adapts to your strengths and weaknesses
- Schedules optimal review times based on forgetting curves

Khan Academy:
- Implements AI-powered mastery learning
- Provides personalized recommendations and practice
- Offers targeted interventions when students struggle

Coursera:
- Uses AI to match learners with appropriate courses
- Provides personalized assignment feedback
- Offers content recommendations based on career goals

Quizlet:
- Utilizes spaced repetition algorithms
- Adapts flashcards and quizzes to your learning needs
- Predicts which concepts you're likely to forget

DIY AI Learning Assistant

You can create your own personalized learning system using general AI tools:

Step 1: Create a Learning Plan
161.   Tell ChatGPT or Claude what you want to learn
162.   Ask it to create a structured learning path with milestones
163.   Request resource recommendations for each stage

Step 2: Generate Learning Materials
164.   Ask your AI assistant to create summaries of key concepts
165.   Request practice questions at various difficulty levels
166.   Have it generate examples that relate to your interests or work

Step 3: Implement Active Recall
167.   Use your AI assistant to quiz you on material you've learned
168.   Ask it to explain concepts you're struggling with in different ways
169.   Request increasingly challenging questions as you progress

Step 4: Track and Adapt
170.   Regularly review your progress with your AI assistant
171.   Ask it to identify areas needing more focus
172.   Have it adjust your learning plan based on your progress

This approach gives you the benefits of personalized learning without requiring specialized platforms.

Skill Development with AI Coaches

Beyond formal learning, AI can help you develop practical skills through personalized coaching and feedback.

AI as Your Personal Coach

AI coaching can support skill development in several ways:

Structured Practice:
- Creating customized practice routines
- Scaling difficulty based on your current level
- Providing variety to maintain engagement

Feedback and Correction:
- Analyzing your performance or output
- Identifying specific areas for improvement
- Suggesting alternative approaches or techniques

Motivation and Accountability:
- Setting appropriate goals and milestones
- Tracking progress over time
- Providing encouragement and maintaining momentum

Skill Categories Benefiting from AI Coaching

AI coaching can be applied to a wide range of skills:

Writing:
- Grammar and style improvement
- Structure and clarity enhancement
- Genre-specific writing techniques

Public Speaking:
- Content organization and delivery
- Voice modulation and pacing
- Addressing filler words and hesitations

Programming:
- Coding practice and challenges
- Code review and optimization
- Learning new languages or frameworks

Business Skills:
- Negotiation tactics and practice
- Leadership and management techniques
- Strategic thinking and problem-solving

Creative Arts:
- Technique development in music, art, or writing
- Style analysis and experimentation
- Project planning and execution

Practical AI Coaching Techniques

Here's how to leverage AI for skill development:

1. Writing Improvement:

To enhance your writing skills:

173. Share your written work with ChatGPT or Claude
174. Ask: "Please analyze this writing and suggest improvements for clarity, structure, and engagement"
175. Request specific feedback on elements like introductions, transitions, or conclusions
176. Ask for before/after examples to illustrate improvements

2. Presentation Skills Development:

To improve your presentations:

177. Share your presentation script or outline
178. Ask: "How can I make this presentation more engaging and impactful?"
179. Request feedback on structure, storytelling, and memorable moments
180. Ask for suggested delivery techniques for key points

3. Problem-Solving Skills Enhancement:

To develop better problem-solving:
181. Present a challenge you're facing to your AI assistant
182. Ask it to guide you through different problem-solving frameworks
183. Request questions that challenge your assumptions
184. Ask for practice scenarios similar to your real-world challenges

Creating Deliberate Practice Plans

For any skill you want to develop, AI can help design effective practice:

Skill Assessment:
- Discuss your current skill level with your AI assistant
- Ask for help identifying strengths and weaknesses
- Request a baseline evaluation framework

Practice Design:
- Ask for specific exercises targeting your weak areas
- Request a progressive difficulty curve
- Seek variety in practice approaches to build well-rounded skills

Feedback Loops:

- Share your practice results with your AI assistant
- Ask for specific, actionable feedback
- Request adjustments to your practice plan based on progress

By utilizing AI in this structured way, you can create a personalized skill development system similar to working with a human coach.

Creative Enhancement with AI Tools

Creativity is no longer the exclusive domain of "creative types." AI tools can help anyone enhance their creative capabilities and produce impressive creative work.

AI as a Creative Partner

AI can support creativity in several ways:

Idea Generation:
- Producing novel combinations and connections
- Offering unexpected perspectives
- Exploring variations on themes

Creative Expansion:
- Developing initial concepts further
- Suggesting alternative approaches
- Building upon existing elements

Creative Constraints:
- Providing productive limitations to focus creativity
- Suggesting unusual requirements or parameters

- Creating "creative prompts" to spark new thinking

Creative Domains Enhanced by AI

AI creative tools span various domains:

Written Creativity:
- Story plots and character development
- Poetry and lyric generation
- Creative non-fiction approaches

Visual Art:
- Style exploration and experimentation
- Composition and design alternatives
- Visual concept development

Music:
- Melody and harmony generation
- Style fusion and experimentation
- Arrangement and orchestration options

Design:
- Layout alternatives and variations
- Color scheme exploration
- Typography and visual hierarchy options

Mixed Media:
- Combining text and visuals in novel ways
- Creating multimedia narrative experiences
- Developing cross-platform creative concepts

Practical Creative Enhancement Techniques

Here's how to use AI to boost your creativity:

1. Creative Writing Enhancement:

To develop your creative writing:
185. Share your initial concept or draft with your AI assistant
186. Ask: "What are some unexpected directions I could take this story?"
187. Request character development suggestions or plot complications
188. Ask for stylistic variations of key passages

2. Visual Concept Development:

To explore visual ideas:
189. Describe your basic concept to an image generation AI
190. Experiment with different styles, settings, and elements
191. Use the generated images as inspiration rather than final products
192. Iterate based on what aspects resonate with you

3. Creative Problem-Solving:

To find innovative solutions:
193. Explain a challenge to your AI assistant
194. Ask: "What are 10 unconventional approaches to solving this problem?"
195. Request combinations of different solution elements
196. Ask for evaluation of the most promising ideas

Overcoming Creative Blocks

AI is particularly valuable for breaking through creative blocks:

Constraint Introduction:
- Ask your AI assistant to provide random constraints or requirements
- Use these limitations to force creative thinking
- Combine unexpected elements suggested by the AI

Perspective Shifting:
- Request that your AI reframe your problem from different viewpoints
- Ask for interpretations from various disciplines or domains
- Explore how different personas might approach your challenge

Divergent Thinking Exercises:
- Ask your AI assistant to generate unusual associations
- Request metaphors and analogies for your concept
- Use these connections as springboards for new ideas

Remember that the goal is not to have AI create for you, but to enhance your creative processes and capabilities through collaboration with AI tools.

Health and Wellness Applications

AI can also support your physical and mental wellbeing through personalized guidance, tracking, and intervention.

AI for Physical Health

AI tools can help you optimize various aspects of physical health:

Personalized Exercise Recommendations:
- Customized workout plans based on your goals and constraints
- Form analysis and correction guidance
- Progressive adaptation as your fitness improves

Nutrition Optimization:
- Meal planning tailored to your dietary preferences and goals
- Nutritional analysis of your current diet
- Personalized recommendations for improvements

Sleep Improvement:
- Analysis of sleep patterns and quality
- Personalized recommendations for better sleep
- Tracking of interventions and their effectiveness

AI for Mental Wellbeing

Mental health is another area benefiting from AI support:

Mood Tracking and Analysis:
- Identifying patterns in mood fluctuations
- Correlating activities with emotional states
- Suggesting interventions based on patterns

Stress Management:
- Personalized meditation and mindfulness guidance
- Stress trigger identification
- Adaptive coping strategy recommendations

Cognitive Support:
- Cognitive behavioral therapy techniques
- Thought pattern recognition and reframing
- Progressive mental resilience building

Practical Health and Wellness Techniques

Here's how to use AI for health improvements:

1. Personalized Workout Planning:

To create a fitness plan:
197.   Share your fitness goals, available equipment, and time constraints with your AI assistant
198.   Ask: "Can you create a 4-week progressive workout plan that fits these parameters?"
199.   Request modifications for days when you have less time
200.   Ask for form cues and technique tips for each exercise

2. Meal Planning and Nutrition:

For dietary optimization:
201.   Share your dietary preferences, restrictions, and goals
202.   Ask your AI assistant to create a weekly meal plan with shopping list
203.   Request nutritional analysis of your favorite recipes
204.   Ask for simple modifications to improve nutritional value

3. Stress Reduction Techniques:

For better stress management:
205.   Describe your common stress triggers to your AI assistant
206.   Ask for personalized stress reduction techniques

207.   Request a progressive plan to build stress resilience
208.   Ask for quick interventions for acute stress situations

Building Sustainable Health Habits

AI can help you develop lasting health habits:

Habit Formation Support:
- Ask your AI assistant to help design tiny habits that lead to larger changes
- Request implementation intention formulations ("When X happens, I will do Y")
- Create environment modification strategies to support habit formation

Progress Tracking:
- Develop simple tracking systems for your key health metrics
- Ask your AI to help analyze patterns in your data
- Request adjustments based on what's working and what isn't

Motivation Maintenance:
- Use your AI assistant to generate personalized motivational content
- Create rewarding milestone celebrations
- Develop strategies for overcoming common obstacles

The key is using AI to personalize health approaches to your specific needs, preferences, and challenges, rather than following generic advice.

Building Personal Knowledge Management Systems

In our information-rich world, organizing what you know and learn is increasingly valuable. AI can help you build effective personal knowledge management systems.

The Components of Knowledge Management

Effective personal knowledge systems typically include:

Information Capture:
- Collecting relevant information from various sources
- Processing and initially categorizing new information
- Extracting key ideas and concepts

Organization and Connection:
- Structuring information in accessible ways
- Creating links between related concepts
- Building a network of knowledge rather than isolated facts

Retrieval and Application:
- Finding the right information when needed
- Applying knowledge to new situations
- Identifying gaps and areas for expansion

AI-Enhanced Knowledge Management Tools

Several tools leverage AI for better knowledge management:

Notion AI:
- Helps organize and connect your notes and documents
- Provides AI-powered summaries and extractions
- Allows natural language queries of your knowledge base

Obsidian:
- Facilitates connection-building between notes
- Can be enhanced with AI plugins for analysis and suggestion
- Supports knowledge visualization and exploration

Mem.ai:
- Automatically connects related information
- Provides AI-powered search and discovery
- Suggests connections you might have missed

Roam Research:
- Supports bidirectional linking for network building
- Offers AI extensions for knowledge processing
- Facilitates emergent structure in your knowledge

Building Your AI-Powered Knowledge System

Here's how to create an effective personal knowledge management system:

Step 1: Capture System Setup
209. Choose a primary tool for information storage (Notion, Obsidian, etc.)
210. Develop simple templates for different types of information
211. Create frictionless capture methods for quick ideas and findings

Step 2: Processing Workflow

212. Use AI to summarize lengthy content
213. Ask your AI assistant to extract key concepts and ideas
214. Have AI suggest connections to existing knowledge
215. Use AI to convert information into your preferred format

Step 3: Organization Framework
216. Develop a flexible categorization system
217. Create both hierarchical and network-based organization
218. Use AI to suggest improvements to your organizational structure
219. Implement regular review and refinement sessions

Step 4: Retrieval Enhancement
220. Use AI to create comprehensive indices
221. Develop natural language query capabilities
222. Create AI-powered dashboards for different knowledge contexts
223. Implement spaced repetition for important information

From Information to Personal Expertise

The goal of knowledge management is transforming information into expertise:

Concept Mastery:
- Use AI to create explanations at multiple levels of complexity
- Ask your AI assistant to generate practice questions for key concepts
- Create connections between new knowledge and existing expertise

Application Development:
- Ask AI to suggest practical applications of theoretical knowledge

- Create scenario-based thought experiments
- Develop templates for applying knowledge to different contexts

Knowledge Synthesis:
- Use AI to help combine ideas from different domains
- Ask for comparisons and contrasts between related concepts
- Create personal "mental models" for complex systems

By building a systematic approach to knowledge management with AI assistance, you can dramatically increase your learning efficiency and retention.

Practical Activity: Create Your AI Learning Plan

Now it's time to apply what you've learned by creating a personalized learning and development plan with AI assistance.

Project: Design a Personal Growth System

Step 1: Growth Area Identification
224.   Identify 1-3 areas where you want to grow (skills, knowledge, health, etc.)
225.   For each area, define:
- Your current level (beginner, intermediate, advanced)
- Your specific goals and desired outcomes
- Your available time and resources
- Your preferred learning methods

Step 2: Learning Resource Curation

226.   Use your AI assistant to help identify optimal learning resources:
    - Ask: "What are the best resources for learning [your topic] at my level?"
    - Request a mix of formats (books, courses, videos, practice exercises)
    - Ask for recommendations prioritized by quality and relevance

Step 3: Structured Learning Plan Creation

227.   Work with your AI assistant to create a detailed learning plan:
    - Ask for a week-by-week curriculum
    - Request milestone definitions and progress markers
    - Ask for specific activities and assignments
    - Have AI suggest how to balance theory and practice

Step 4: Practice and Feedback System Design

228.   Design a system for deliberate practice:
    - Ask AI to create practice activities for different skills
    - Request feedback frameworks for self-assessment
    - Develop methods for tracking improvement
    - Create templates for reflection and adjustment

Step 5: Implementation and Tracking Strategy

229.   Develop a practical implementation approach:
    - Create a schedule with specific time blocks
    - Design a simple tracking system for progress
    - Plan for regular reviews and adjustments
    - Identify potential obstacles and solutions

Reflection Questions:

- How does this AI-assisted learning plan differ from approaches you've tried before?
- What aspects of your plan feel most exciting and motivating?

- What potential challenges might you face in implementing this plan?
- How will you measure success in your learning journey?

By completing this activity, you'll have created a comprehensive personal growth system tailored to your specific needs and goals, with AI as your learning partner.

Day 6 Summary

Today, we've explored how AI can enhance your personal growth and development:
- AI-powered learning platforms that personalize educational experiences
- Skill development with AI coaches providing feedback and guidance
- Creative enhancement using AI as a collaborative partner
- Health and wellness applications for physical and mental wellbeing
- Building personal knowledge management systems with AI assistance
- Creating a comprehensive AI learning plan for ongoing growth

You now have the knowledge to leverage AI for continuous personal improvement across multiple dimensions of your life.

Tomorrow's Preview: On our final day, Day 7, we'll focus on staying ahead of AI trends. You'll learn about emerging AI capabilities, ethical considerations, how AI will transform various careers, and how to develop your personal AI skill roadmap. This forward-looking exploration will help you continue your AI journey well beyond this book.

Excellent progress today! You've gained valuable insights into how AI can support your personal development journey.

Welcome to Day 7, the final day of your AI mastery journey! Over the past six days, we've explored how AI can enhance various aspects of your life and work, from productivity and decision-making to creativity and personal growth. Today, we'll focus on the future – how to stay ahead of rapidly evolving AI trends, understand emerging capabilities, navigate ethical considerations, and adapt your career to thrive in an AI-enhanced world.

The Future of No-Code AI

No-code AI has already democratized access to artificial intelligence, but this is just the beginning. Let's explore where this technology is headed and how you can stay at the forefront.

Emerging Capabilities in No-Code AI

The no-code AI landscape is evolving rapidly with several key trends:

Increased Sophistication with Simplified Interfaces:
- Tools are becoming more powerful while getting easier to use
- Complex capabilities are being packaged into intuitive workflows
- Advanced customization is becoming available without technical knowledge

Specialized Domain Tools:
- Industry-specific AI solutions are emerging for fields like healthcare, finance, and education

- These tools incorporate domain expertise directly into their interfaces
- They solve specific problems with minimal configuration required

Multi-Modal Integration:
- Tools are increasingly able to work with multiple types of data (text, images, audio, video)
- Unified platforms are emerging that handle diverse AI tasks
- This allows for more complex and comprehensive AI applications

Automated AI Solution Building:
- Systems that can automatically select and configure appropriate AI approaches
- "AI building AI" where the platform determines the best architecture for your needs
- This removes the need to understand which AI approach fits which problem

Tracking Technological Progress

To stay ahead of these developments:

Following Key Information Sources:
- AI-focused newsletters like "The Algorithm" (MIT Technology Review) and "Import AI"
- Industry blogs from major AI providers (OpenAI, Google, Microsoft, Anthropic)
- Communities like Hugging Face and GitHub where new tools are shared

Understanding Key Metrics:

- Recognizing benchmark improvements that indicate significant advances
- Identifying new capabilities that cross important thresholds
- Noticing when previously complex tasks become accessible to non-experts

Testing New Tools Early:
- Signing up for beta programs from leading AI companies
- Experimenting with new capabilities as they're released
- Building a practice of regular exploration and testing

Preparing for Future Capabilities

Here's how to position yourself for upcoming advances:

Skill Anticipation:
- Identifying which human skills will complement, rather than compete with, advancing AI
- Focusing on areas where human judgment, creativity, and ethical reasoning remain essential
- Developing the ability to effectively direct and leverage AI tools

Use Case Exploration:
- Regularly brainstorming how new AI capabilities could apply to your specific context
- Thinking beyond obvious applications to identify unique opportunities
- Creating a personal "AI roadmap" of capabilities you want to implement when available

Building an Experimentation Mindset:
- Treating new AI tools as opportunities for learning and discovery
- Developing routines for testing and evaluating new capabilities

- Sharing findings and learning from others' experiences

The key is to view AI advancement not as something that happens to you, but as a set of emerging opportunities that you actively engage with and shape to your needs.

Emerging AI Capabilities for Non-Technical Users

Beyond current no-code tools, several emerging capabilities will be particularly valuable for non-technical users in the near future.

Multimodal AI Systems

AI that can work across different types of content simultaneously:

Text-Image-Audio Integration:
- Systems that understand relationships between words, visuals, and sounds
- The ability to generate content that spans multiple formats coherently
- Tools that can convert seamlessly between different content types

Real-World Interaction:
- AI that can interpret and respond to the physical environment
- Systems that bridge the digital and physical worlds
- Tools that understand context beyond digital content

Practical Applications:

- Creating comprehensive multimedia content from simple prompts
- Building presentations that automatically align visuals with script
- Developing interactive materials that adapt to different learning styles

Personalized AI Agents

AI systems that act autonomously on your behalf:

Personal AI Assistants:
- Systems that learn your preferences and working style
- AI that can anticipate your needs based on context
- Assistants that handle routine tasks with minimal oversight

Domain-Specific Agents:
- Specialized AI for different aspects of your life (work, learning, health)
- Systems with deep knowledge in particular fields
- Agents that can interact with other systems on your behalf

Collaborative AI Teams:
- Multiple AI systems working together on complex tasks
- Different specialized agents contributing their capabilities
- Coordinated efforts managed through natural language direction

Human-AI Collaboration Models

New ways of working with AI as a partner:

Conversation-Based Creation:

- Creating complex projects through natural dialogue with AI
- Iterative refinement through discussion rather than technical inputs
- Collaborative problem-solving with AI suggesting alternatives

AI-Enhanced Decision Making:

- Systems that present options with clear tradeoffs
- AI that can explain its reasoning in non-technical terms
- Tools that help you explore the implications of different choices

Continuous Learning Relationships:

- AI that improves based on your feedback and preferences
- Systems that adapt to your evolving needs and skills
- Long-term collaborative relationships that become more valuable over time

Preparing for These Capabilities

To make the most of these emerging technologies:

Develop Clear Mental Models:

- Understand the basic principles behind these capabilities
- Form realistic expectations about possibilities and limitations
- Identify where these technologies could address your specific challenges

Build Effective Collaboration Skills:

- Practice clear communication with AI systems
- Learn to provide helpful feedback and direction
- Develop the ability to evaluate AI outputs critically

Think Systemically:

- Consider how different AI capabilities could work together
- Identify workflows where multiple AI tools could create synergies
- Design processes that leverage both human and AI strengths

By understanding these emerging capabilities, you'll be better positioned to adopt and benefit from them as they become available to non-technical users.

AI Ethics and Responsible Use

As AI becomes more powerful and integrated into daily life, understanding ethical considerations becomes increasingly important. Responsible use ensures that AI enhances human potential rather than undermining important values.

Key Ethical Considerations

Several ethical dimensions are particularly relevant for everyday AI users:

Privacy and Data Protection:
- Understanding what information AI systems collect and store
- Recognizing the privacy implications of different AI tools
- Making informed decisions about data sharing

Accuracy and Reliability:
- Recognizing that AI systems can produce incorrect information confidently
- Understanding the importance of verification and human oversight

- Being aware of when to trust and when to verify AI outputs

Bias and Fairness:
- Recognizing that AI systems can reflect and amplify societal biases
- Understanding how training data influences AI behavior
- Identifying potentially biased outputs and correcting for them

Transparency and Explainability:
- Knowing when you have the right to understand how decisions are made
- Recognizing the difference between explainable and "black box" systems
- Asking appropriate questions about how AI reaches conclusions

Environmental Impact:
- Being aware of the energy consumption of different AI approaches
- Understanding the resource implications of AI use
- Making informed choices about when AI use is justified

Practical Framework for Ethical AI Use

Here's a simple framework for making ethical decisions about AI use:

1. Purpose Assessment:
- What problem am I trying to solve with AI?
- Is AI the appropriate solution for this problem?
- Are my intentions aligned with positive outcomes for all stakeholders?

2. Impact Evaluation:

- Who might be affected by this AI application?
- What are the potential positive and negative impacts?
- Are the benefits distributed fairly?

3. Risk Mitigation:
- What could go wrong with this AI application?
- How can I verify outputs and ensure quality?
- What safeguards or oversight should I implement?

4. Transparency Commitment:
- Am I being open about how AI is being used?
- Do people interacting with this AI understand its role?
- Have I disclosed AI use where appropriate?

5. Continuous Review:
- How will I monitor this AI system's performance?
- What feedback mechanisms will I use?
- When will I reevaluate whether this use of AI is still appropriate?

Responsible Use Guidelines

Here are specific guidelines for different contexts:

Personal Use:
- Be mindful of the data you share with AI systems
- Verify important information from AI sources
- Consider the impact on others when sharing AI-generated content

Professional Use:
- Disclose AI use to colleagues and clients where appropriate
- Maintain human oversight of important decisions
- Document AI processes for transparency and accountability

Creative Use:
- Respect intellectual property considerations
- Acknowledge AI assistance where relevant
- Use AI to augment rather than replace human creativity

Educational Use:
- Teach critical evaluation of AI outputs
- Balance AI assistance with skill development
- Use AI to enhance rather than shortcut learning

By incorporating these ethical considerations into your AI use, you'll ensure that your adoption of this technology remains responsible and aligned with human values.

How AI Will Transform Jobs (And Create New Ones)

AI is already changing the employment landscape, but contrary to some fears, it's creating as many opportunities as challenges. Understanding these shifts will help you position yourself advantageously.

AI's Impact on Work

AI is affecting different types of work in different ways:

Automatable Tasks:
- Routine, rule-based activities are increasingly automated
- Tasks requiring predictable physical movements
- Basic data processing and analysis

Augmented Tasks:
- Complex decision-making enhanced by AI insights
- Creative work supported by AI suggestions
- Specialized knowledge augmented by AI information retrieval

New Task Categories:
- AI oversight and management
- Human-AI collaboration design
- Ethical evaluation of AI applications

Emerging AI-Related Roles

Many new positions are emerging that don't require technical expertise:

AI Prompt Engineer:
- Crafting effective instructions for AI systems
- Optimizing queries to get the best results
- Translating business needs into effective AI directions

AI Implementation Specialist:
- Identifying opportunities for AI application
- Selecting appropriate AI tools for specific challenges
- Managing the integration of AI into workflows

AI Ethics Consultant:
- Evaluating the ethical implications of AI use
- Developing guidelines for responsible AI adoption
- Ensuring AI implementations align with organizational values

AI-Human Experience Designer:
- Creating effective interfaces between humans and AI

- Designing workflows that leverage both human and AI strengths
- Optimizing the collaboration between people and AI systems

AI Content Strategist:
- Developing strategies for AI-assisted content creation
- Ensuring brand consistency across AI-generated materials
- Balancing automation with human creativity

AI-Proofing Your Career

Here's how to ensure your career thrives in an AI-enhanced world:

Develop Complementary Skills:
- Emotional intelligence and interpersonal communication
- Creative problem-solving and innovation
- Ethical reasoning and critical thinking
- Strategic vision and systems thinking

Position Yourself as an AI Translator:
- Build the ability to bridge technical and non-technical domains
- Develop skills in explaining AI capabilities to non-experts
- Learn to translate business problems into AI opportunities

Focus on Human-AI Collaboration:
- Master the art of directing AI effectively
- Develop workflows that combine human and AI strengths
- Build expertise in reviewing and refining AI outputs

Continuous Learning Orientation:
- Commit to regular upskilling as AI capabilities evolve
- Develop learning routines that keep pace with technology
- Build networks that share knowledge about emerging trends

AI and Entrepreneurship

AI is creating unprecedented opportunities for entrepreneurship:

Niche Service Businesses:
- Specialized AI implementation for specific industries
- Custom AI solution development for particular needs
- AI training and change management consulting

AI-Enabled Products:
- Creating unique products enhanced by AI capabilities
- Developing specialized AI agents for particular purposes
- Building businesses that combine AI with human expertise

AI Augmented Creative Services:
- Offering enhanced creative services using AI tools
- Providing high-quality, AI-assisted content creation
- Developing unique creative processes that leverage AI

The most successful approach to AI and careers isn't to compete with AI or ignore it, but to become skilled at leveraging it to create new value in ways that weren't previously possible.

Building an AI-Enhanced Career in Any Field

Let's explore how AI is transforming specific professions and how you can leverage AI within your particular field.

AI Across Industries

AI is impacting virtually every profession, but in different ways:

Marketing and Communications:
- Content generation and personalization
- Customer behavior analysis and prediction
- Campaign optimization and testing

Education and Training:
- Personalized learning experiences
- Automated assessment and feedback
- Custom resource creation and adaptation

Healthcare and Wellness:
- Diagnosis assistance and treatment planning
- Patient engagement and monitoring
- Administrative efficiency and documentation

Finance and Accounting:
- Financial analysis and forecasting
- Fraud detection and risk assessment
- Automated reporting and compliance

Creative and Design:
- Concept generation and exploration
- Design variation and testing
- Production automation and enhancement

Customer Service:
- Intelligent routing and prioritization
- Response assistance and quality monitoring
- Proactive issue resolution

Field-Specific AI Strategies

For your specific field, consider this approach:

Step 1: Capability Assessment
- Identify which AI tools are most relevant to your field
- Determine which aspects of your work could benefit from AI
- Research how early adopters in your industry are using AI

Step 2: Value Creation Mapping
- Identify where AI could help you create unique value
- Determine how AI could enhance your particular strengths
- Find opportunities to combine your expertise with AI capabilities

Step 3: Skill Development Planning
- Identify which AI-related skills are most valuable in your field
- Determine how to build those skills incrementally
- Create a learning plan that aligns with your career goals

Step 4: Positioning Strategy
- Decide how to communicate your AI capabilities to employers or clients
- Determine how to demonstrate the value of your AI-enhanced work
- Create a narrative about how you uniquely combine human expertise with AI tools

Practical Activity: Develop Your AI Skill Roadmap

Now it's time to apply what you've learned by creating a personalized AI skill roadmap that will guide your continued growth after completing this book.

Project: Your Personal AI Development Plan

Step 1: Current State Assessment

230.   Evaluate your current AI capabilities:
- Which AI tools are you comfortable using?
- What AI-related concepts do you understand?
- How effectively are you currently using AI in your work or life?

231.   Identify your starting position:
- Beginner: Just starting to explore AI tools
- Intermediate: Comfortable with basic tools but want to expand
- Advanced: Already using multiple AI tools and ready to deepen expertise

Step 2: Goal Definition

232.   Define your AI learning goals:
- What do you want to be able to accomplish with AI?
- How do you want AI to enhance your career or personal life?
- What specific outcomes would indicate success?

233.   Create specific, measurable objectives:
- Tools you want to master
- Applications you want to implement
- Problems you want to solve using AI

Step 3: Skill Identification

234.   Based on your goals, identify key skills to develop:
- Tool-specific skills (e.g., advanced prompt engineering)

- Process skills (e.g., AI integration into workflows)
- Evaluation skills (e.g., quality assessment of AI outputs)

235. Prioritize these skills based on:
   - Impact on your goals
   - Building block relationships (prerequisites)
   - Difficulty and learning curve

Step 4: Learning Resource Identification

236. For each priority skill, identify learning resources:
   - Online courses and tutorials
   - Books and articles
   - Communities and forums
   - Practice opportunities

237. Evaluate resources based on:
   - Quality and comprehensiveness
   - Learning style compatibility
   - Time and cost considerations

Step 5: Timeline and Milestones

238. Create a realistic timeline for skill development:
   - Short-term goals (1-3 months)
   - Medium-term goals (3-6 months)
   - Long-term goals (6-12 months)

239. Define specific milestones to track progress:
   - Completion of learning modules
   - Implementation of specific AI applications
   - Measurable improvements in productivity or capabilities

Step 6: Implementation Strategy

240. Design a practical implementation approach:
   - Regular learning sessions
   - Practice projects

- Feedback mechanisms
- Accountability systems

241.   Address potential obstacles:
- Time constraints
- Resource limitations
- Knowledge gaps
- Motivation challenges

Reflection Questions:
- How does this AI skill roadmap align with your broader career or life goals?
- What potential challenges might you face in implementing this plan?
- How will you know if you're making progress toward your AI mastery goals?
- What support or resources might you need to succeed?

By completing this activity, you'll have a comprehensive plan for continuing your AI journey well beyond this book, ensuring that you stay ahead of trends and continue building valuable skills.

Day 7 Summary

Today, we've explored how to stay ahead in the rapidly evolving world of AI:
- Understanding the future of no-code AI and emerging capabilities
- Considering ethical dimensions and frameworks for responsible AI use
- Recognizing how AI is transforming jobs and creating new opportunities
- Building field-specific strategies for AI-enhanced careers

- Creating your personal AI skill roadmap for continued growth

You now have the knowledge and perspective needed to navigate the AI landscape as it continues to evolve, ensuring that you can adapt to changes and leverage new capabilities as they emerge.

Conclusion: Your AI Journey Has Just Begun

Congratulations on completing our 7-day AI mastery journey! Over the past week, you've transformed from an AI novice to someone who understands how to leverage artificial intelligence in numerous aspects of your life and work – all without writing a single line of code.

Let's recap what you've accomplished:

Day 1: You built a foundation by understanding AI fundamentals, key concepts, and how AI already impacts your daily life.

Day 2: You explored no-code AI tools and platforms, setting up your personal AI toolkit and creating your first AI project.

Day 3: You discovered the creative potential of generative AI across text, images, video, and audio formats.

Day 4: You learned how to boost your productivity through AI-powered automation, research, document analysis, and workflow optimization.

Day 5: You developed skills for using AI to make better decisions through data analysis, market research, customer insights, and forecasting.

Day 6: You explored how AI can enhance your personal growth through learning, skill development, creativity, health management, and knowledge organization.

Day 7: You gained perspective on future AI trends, ethical considerations, career implications, and created your personal AI skill roadmap.

The Path Forward

As you continue your AI journey, remember these key principles:

Continuous Exploration:
- The AI landscape is evolving rapidly
- Regular experimentation with new tools and capabilities is essential
- Staying curious and open to new possibilities will serve you well

Balanced Perspective:
- AI is a powerful tool, but not a replacement for human judgment
- The most effective approach combines AI capabilities with human strengths
- Critical thinking about AI outputs remains essential

Ethical Mindfulness:
- With great power comes great responsibility
- Consider the broader implications of your AI applications
- Contribute to the development of responsible AI use in your sphere

Collaborative Orientation:
- Share your AI discoveries and insights with others
- Learn from diverse perspectives on AI applications

- Build communities of practice around effective AI use

Final Thoughts

The democratization of AI through no-code tools represents one of the most significant technological transformations of our time. You are now positioned to be part of this revolution – not as a passive recipient of technology, but as an active participant who shapes how AI is used to create value and solve problems.

Remember that mastery is an ongoing journey. Each new AI capability you explore, each application you implement, and each lesson you learn builds upon your foundation. The skills you've developed through this book are just the beginning of what's possible as you continue to grow and adapt alongside this transformative technology.

Thank you for embarking on this journey. Now go forth and use your new AI capabilities to enhance your life, advance your career, and create positive impact in your world!

This bonus section provides a comprehensive collection of resources to support your ongoing AI journey. Here you'll find a curated directory of AI tools organized by category, recommended learning resources, communities to join, and additional guidance for continued growth.

AI Tool Directory

Conversational AI and Large Language Models

These general-purpose AI assistants can help with a wide range of tasks through natural language interaction:

ChatGPT (OpenAI)
- Website: chat.openai.com
- Free tier: GPT-3.5
- Paid tier: GPT-4
- Best for: Writing, research, brainstorming, coding assistance, learning, general problem-solving

Claude (Anthropic)
- Website: claude.ai
- Free tier: Claude 2
- Paid tier: Claude 3 (Opus and Sonnet)
- Best for: Detailed analysis, nuanced writing, document processing, thoughtful explanations

Gemini (Google)
- Website: gemini.google.com
- Free tier: Gemini 1.0
- Paid tier: Gemini Advanced
- Best for: Research, real-time information, integration with Google tools, code assistance

Perplexity
- Website: perplexity.ai
- Free tier: Available
- Paid tier: Pro version
- Best for: Research with web search integration, summarizing information, up-to-date answers

Text and Writing Tools

Specialized tools for various writing and text processing tasks:

Grammarly
- Website: grammarly.com
- Free tier: Basic grammar checking
- Paid tier: Advanced features
- Best for: Grammar correction, tone adjustment, clarity improvements

Wordtune
- Website: wordtune.com
- Free tier: Limited rewrites
- Paid tier: Full features
- Best for: Sentence rewording, tone changes, length adjustments

Rytr
- Website: rytr.me
- Free tier: Limited usage
- Paid tier: Higher usage limits
- Best for: Marketing copy, emails, blog posts, creative writing

Jasper
- Website: jasper.ai
- Free trial: Available
- Paid tier: Required for continued use
- Best for: Marketing content, long-form content, templates for specific content types

Image Generation and Design

Tools that create and edit images using AI:

DALL-E (OpenAI)
- Access: Via ChatGPT and dalle.com
- Free tier: Limited generations
- Paid tier: More generations
- Best for: Creating photorealistic or artistic images from text descriptions

Midjourney
- Access: Via Discord
- Free tier: Limited trial
- Paid tier: Required for continued use
- Best for: Highly artistic, stylized images with exceptional quality

Canva Magic Studio
- Website: canva.com
- Free tier: Basic features
- Paid tier: Advanced features
- Best for: Marketing materials, social media graphics, presentations with AI assistance

Leonardo.ai
- Website: leonardo.ai
- Free tier: Limited generations
- Paid tier: More generations and features
- Best for: Character design, concept art, style customization

Video Creation and Editing

Tools for generating and editing video content:

Synthesia

- Website: synthesia.io
- Free trial: Limited
- Paid tier: Required for continued use
- Best for: Creating videos with AI avatars, professional presentations, training content

RunwayML
- Website: runwayml.com
- Free tier: Limited features
- Paid tier: Full access
- Best for: Video editing, special effects, style transfer, text-to-video

HeyGen
- Website: heygen.com
- Free trial: Available
- Paid tier: Required for continued use
- Best for: AI avatar videos, professional presentations, multilingual content

Descript
- Website: descript.com
- Free tier: Limited features
- Paid tier: Full access
- Best for: Video editing through text editing, transcription, audio enhancement

Audio Generation and Processing

Tools for creating and editing audio content:

ElevenLabs
- Website: elevenlabs.io

- Free tier: Limited usage
- Paid tier: More voices and usage
- Best for: Natural text-to-speech, voice cloning, audiobook creation

Murf

- Website: murf.ai
- Free tier: Limited usage
- Paid tier: More features and usage
- Best for: Voiceovers, presentations, podcast intros, multilingual content

Suno

- Website: suno.ai
- Free tier: Limited generations
- Paid tier: More features
- Best for: Music generation from text descriptions, custom soundtracks

Whisper (OpenAI)

- Access: Via various applications
- Open source: Free to use
- Best for: Accurate speech-to-text transcription, available in many tools

Productivity and Organization

Tools that help automate tasks and organize information:

Notion AI

- Website: notion.so
- Free tier: Limited AI features
- Paid tier: Full AI features

- Best for: Writing, summarizing, brainstorming within your knowledge management system

Mem.ai
- Website: mem.ai
- Free tier: Basic features
- Paid tier: Advanced features
- Best for: Connected note-taking, knowledge management, AI-powered insights

Otter.ai
- Website: otter.ai
- Free tier: Limited transcription
- Paid tier: More features and minutes
- Best for: Meeting transcription, recording, summarization, action item extraction

Zapier
- Website: zapier.com
- Free tier: Limited automations
- Paid tier: More automations
- Best for: Connecting AI tools with other applications, workflow automation

Research and Learning

Tools specifically designed for research and educational purposes:

Elicit
- Website: elicit.org
- Free tier: Available
- Paid tier: Team features

- Best for: Research paper analysis, literature review, academic research

Consensus
- Website: consensus.app
- Free tier: Limited searches
- Paid tier: More searches
- Best for: Scientific research, finding studies on specific topics

Jenni
- Website: jenni.ai
- Free tier: Limited usage
- Paid tier: Full features
- Best for: Academic writing, research paper assistance, citation help

Explainpaper
- Website: explainpaper.com
- Free tier: Available
- Paid tier: Additional features
- Best for: Understanding research papers, simplified explanations of complex content

Business and Analytics

Tools focused on business applications and data analysis:

Akkio
- Website: akkio.com
- Free trial: Available
- Paid tier: Required for continued use
- Best for: No-code predictive analytics, forecasting, business intelligence

Obviously AI

- Website: obviously.ai
- Free tier: Limited predictions
- Paid tier: More features
- Best for: Predictions from spreadsheet data, no-code machine learning

Viable

- Website: viable.fit
- Free trial: Available
- Paid tier: Required for continued use
- Best for: Customer feedback analysis, survey processing, insight extraction

Krisp

- Website: krisp.ai
- Free tier: Limited noise cancellation
- Paid tier: Full features
- Best for: Meeting transcription, noise cancellation, meeting insights

No-Code AI Development

Platforms that allow you to create custom AI solutions without coding:

Microsoft Lobe

- Website: lobe.ai
- Free: Yes
- Best for: Creating custom image recognition models through simple labeling

Teachable Machine (Google)

- Website: teachablemachine.withgoogle.com
- Free: Yes
- Best for: Building simple machine learning models for images, sounds, and poses

MakeML

- Website: makeml.app
- Free tier: Limited projects
- Paid tier: More features
- Best for: Creating computer vision models through annotation

RunwayML

- Website: runwayml.com
- Free tier: Limited usage
- Paid tier: Full access
- Best for: Creative AI applications, multiple AI models in one platform

Learning Resources

Books on AI for Non-Technical Readers

- "The AI Revolution: How Artificial Intelligence Is Changing Our World" by Robin Li
- "Non-Technical Guide to Machine Learning & Artificial Intelligence" by Savvas Chatzichristofis
- "You Look Like a Thing and I Love You" by Janelle Shane
- "The Future Is Faster Than You Think" by Peter H. Diamandis and Steven Kotler
- "The Alignment Problem" by Brian Christian

Online Courses for AI Literacy

- "AI For Everyone" by Andrew Ng (Coursera)
- "Introduction to Artificial Intelligence" (Elements of AI)
- "AI Fundamentals" (LinkedIn Learning)
- "Understanding Artificial Intelligence" (FutureLearn)
- "Practical Deep Learning for Coders" (fast.ai)

Podcasts on AI Trends and Applications

- "Practical AI" - Focused on making artificial intelligence practical and accessible
- "The AI Podcast" by NVIDIA - Interviews with experts about AI applications
- "The TWIML AI Podcast" - This Week in Machine Learning & AI
- "AI in Business" - How AI is transforming various industries
- "The Data Skeptic" - Critical thinking about AI and data science

YouTube Channels for AI Learning

- "Two Minute Papers" - Quick explanations of AI research
- "AI Coffee Break with Letitia" - Accessible explanations of AI concepts
- "Yannic Kilcher" - Explanations of AI research papers
- "Tensorflow" - Official channel with tutorials and updates
- "AI Explained" - Simple explanations of complex AI topics

AI Communities and Forums

General AI Discussion Communities

- Reddit r/ArtificialIntelligence and r/MachineLearning
- Hugging Face Community
- AI Alignment Forum
- Discord servers like "The AI Horde" and "Midjourney Official"

Tool-Specific Communities

- OpenAI Community Forum
- Anthropic Claude Discord
- Midjourney Discord Community
- Stable Diffusion Discord
- Perplexity Discord Community

Professional Networks

- AI LinkedIn Groups
- AI Meetup Groups (local and virtual)
- Women in AI Network
- AI4ALL - Focused on diversity in AI

Staying Updated on AI News and Trends

Newsletters

- "Import AI" by Jack Clark
- "The Algorithm" by MIT Technology Review
- "The Batch" by Andrew Ng
- "Ben's Bites" - Daily AI news
- "Last Week in AI" - Weekly AI news summary

Websites and Blogs

- AITopics.org
- VentureBeat AI section
- TechCrunch AI articles
- The Gradient
- Towards Data Science

Research Aggregators

- Papers With Code
- ArXiv Sanity Preserver
- Google Scholar AI section
- AI Research Insights Newsletter

Ethical AI Resources

Guidelines and Frameworks

- Montreal Declaration for Responsible AI
- Ethics Guidelines for Trustworthy AI (European Commission)
- OECD AI Principles
- Partnership on AI's Best Practices

Organizations Focused on AI Ethics

- AI Ethics Lab
- The Institute for Ethical AI
- The Future of Life Institute
- The AI Now Institute
- Data & Society

Career Development Resources

AI Skills Assessment Tools

- LinkedIn Skill Assessments
- Coursera Skills Benchmarking
- HackerRank AI Challenges
- Kaggle Competitions (for more technical roles)

Resume and Portfolio Building

- Tips for highlighting AI skills for non-technical roles
- Templates for showcasing AI projects
- Guidelines for demonstrating AI proficiency

Job Boards with AI Focus

- AI Jobs Board
- Machine Learning Jobs
- Tech Jobs for Good
- Remote AI
- AngelList AI Startups

Final Tips for Continued AI Mastery

242. **Start Small, Build Gradually**
    - Begin with simple applications in your daily work
    - Build complexity as your confidence grows
    - Celebrate small wins along the way

243. **Learn Through Projects**
    - Apply AI to solve real problems you care about
    - Document your process and learnings
    - Share your projects to get feedback

244. **Build a Personal Learning Network**
    - Connect with others on similar journeys
    - Share resources and discoveries
    - Learn from diverse perspectives

245. **Balance Breadth and Depth**
    - Explore broadly to understand possibilities
    - Go deep in areas most relevant to your goals
    - Recognize the connections between different AI domains

246. **Stay Ethical and Reflective**
    - Regularly consider the implications of your AI use

- Seek diverse perspectives on ethical questions
- Contribute to responsible AI development

Remember, AI mastery is an ongoing journey rather than a destination. By staying curious, practical, and connected to the broader AI community, you'll continue to grow your capabilities and create value through artificial intelligence.

The tools, resources, and communities listed in this directory will evolve over time. Make it a habit to regularly explore new options and update your personal AI toolkit as the landscape continues to advance.